Life in the Middle Ages was full of excitement and adventure. King Arthur and his knights battled dragons.

Queen Guinivere ruled a magnificent castle. You can be part of all the action!

Before you begin your adventure, you have to help create the characters. It's easy. Just follow the step-by-step instructions. And remember: be creative, and have fun!

Field trips to the museum are great. There's so much to see and learn. Like how different life was back in the Middle Ages, when there were princesses, and knights,

and dragons. Boy, that dragon sure looks real. Maybe a little too real?

NO WAY! Where is that dragon going?

Hey! Watch out! There's a fire-breathing dragon loose in the museum!

Step 1

Draw the boxes. Sketch the main outlines. Don't work on details until you're satisfied with the outline.

Step 2

Go to page 6 and pick out a dragon head (or make your own). Draw it in the space left for it. Put lots of scales on the legs and feathers on the body and wings. Practice by finishing this drawing.

NOTE: shading on tail makes it look hard as a shell.

Everyone knows dragons are scary-looking creatures with forked tongues and scaly tails and spikes all over. What does your dragon look like?

Step 1

Put your tracing of the dragon body over one of these heads and sketch in the outlines.

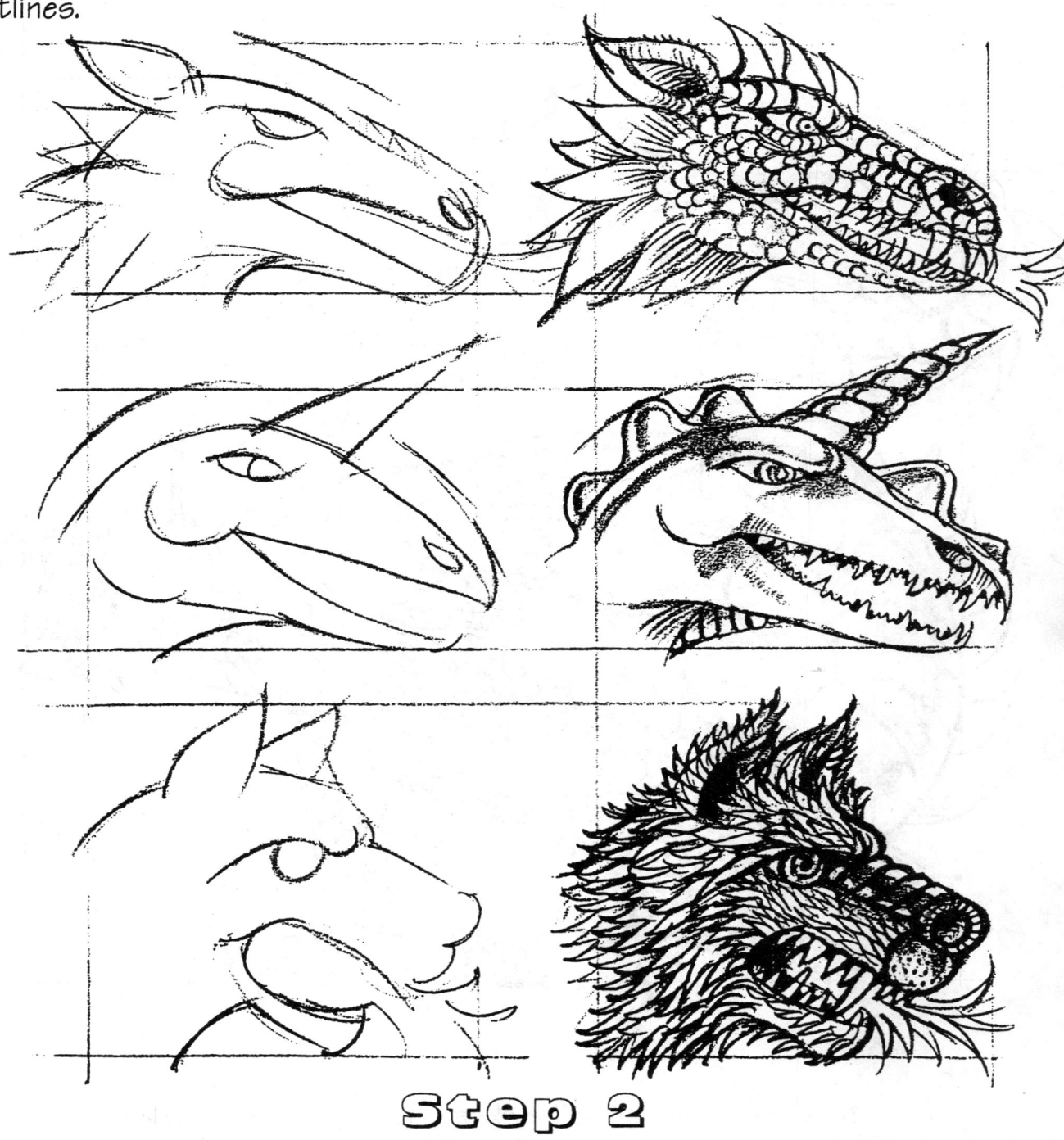

Step 2

Finish the details. Use shading to show hard surfaces like bone. Fire breathing is fun!

Super drawing trick!
How to make a perfectly symmetrical drawing?
(Symmetrical means making sure both sides of your dragon's head have the same shape.)

Step 1
Divide the drawing area in half. Now draw only half of the dragon's face.

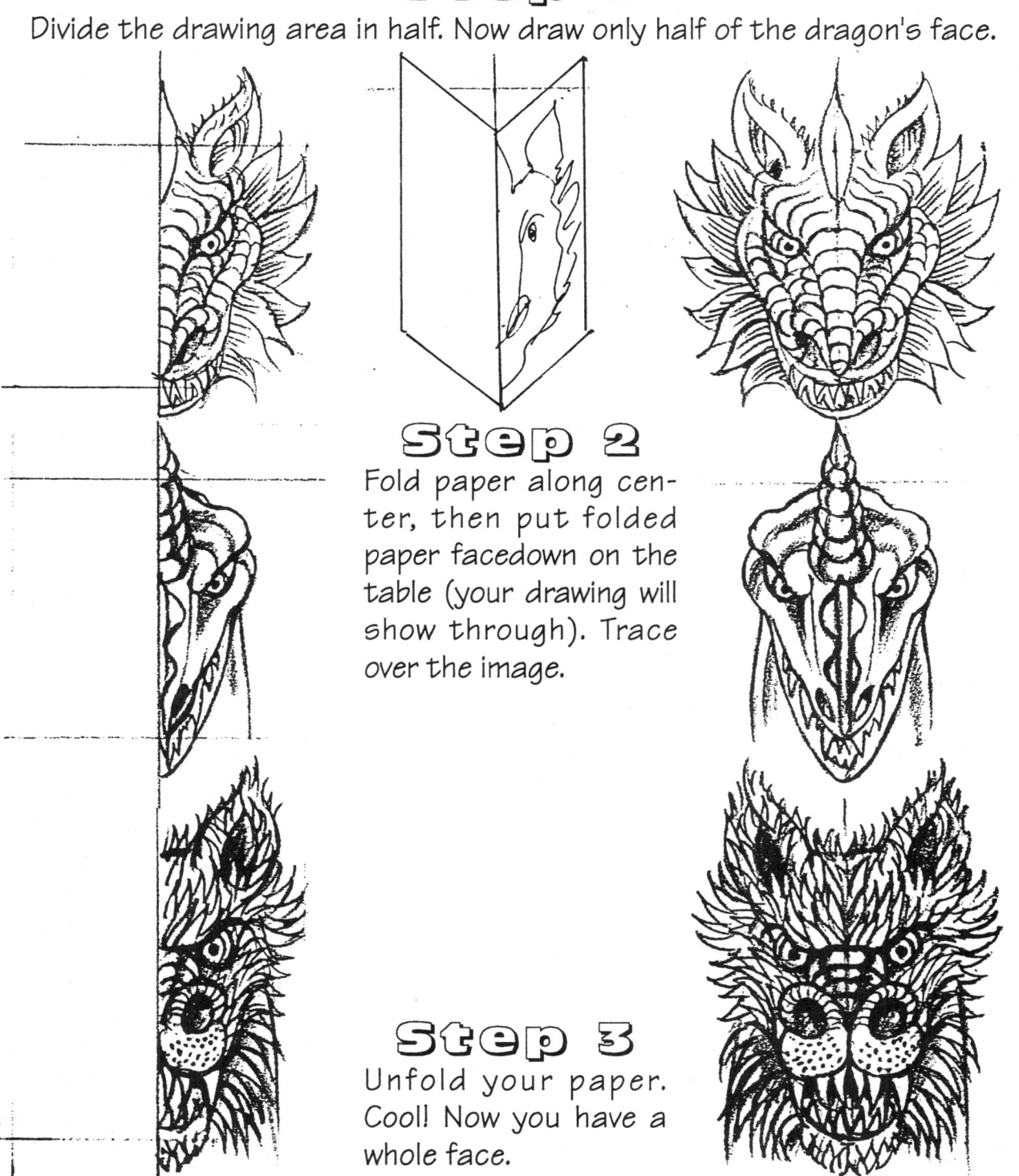

Step 2
Fold paper along center, then put folded paper facedown on the table (your drawing will show through). Trace over the image.

Step 3
Unfold your paper. Cool! Now you have a whole face.

There it is! The fire-breathing dragon. Head on. Face to face. Eyeball to eyeball.

Step 1

Draw a box. Divide it in half. Draw half a dragon on tracing paper. To add a head, put the paper over the front view of the dragon on page 7.

Step 2

Fold your paper in half along center line. (That's the imaginary line that runs down the middle of your paper: it should give you two equal halves.)

Step 3

Trace your drawing. Now unfold the paper. Hey, that was easy! Now add a tail.

How do you fight a dragon? HIDE! (Just kidding. Sort of.)

NOTE: Proportion is like symmetry: it means that one side of your drawing matches the other.

Anyway, if you want to fight that dragon you'll need protection: like a cool suit of armor and a sword!

Each knight had a special helmet. It's how one knight recognized another. Some helmets were fancy with

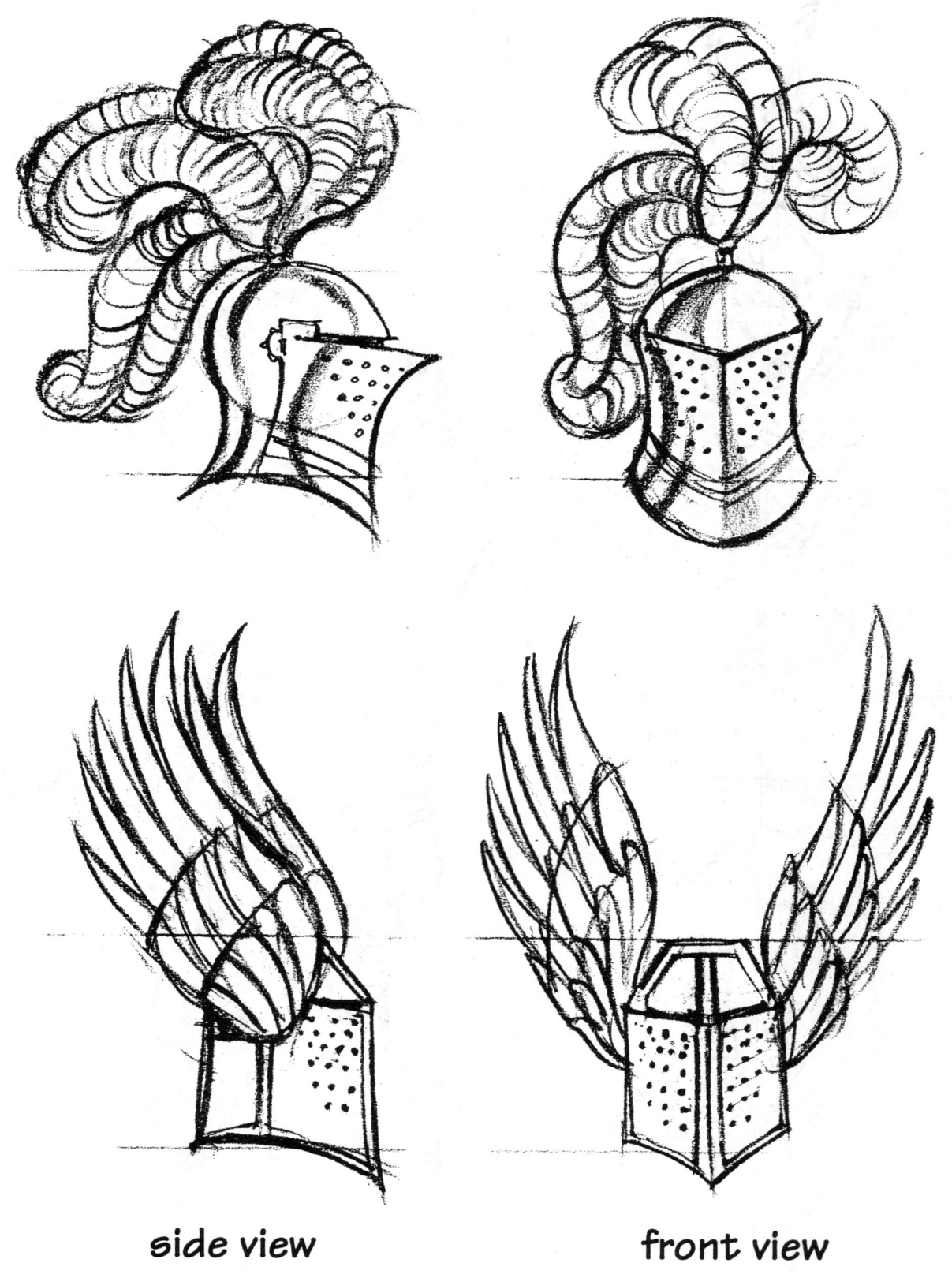

side view   front view

brightly colored plumes. Others were scary with horns or wings or animal heads. But each one was unique.

Here's a wild boar headpiece.

This one looks like a dog.

Helmets and headpieces were very colorful—so experiment and be creative!

OFF WITH YOUR HEAD, DRAGON! No kidding, what dragon wouldn't turn tail and run when you came riding out

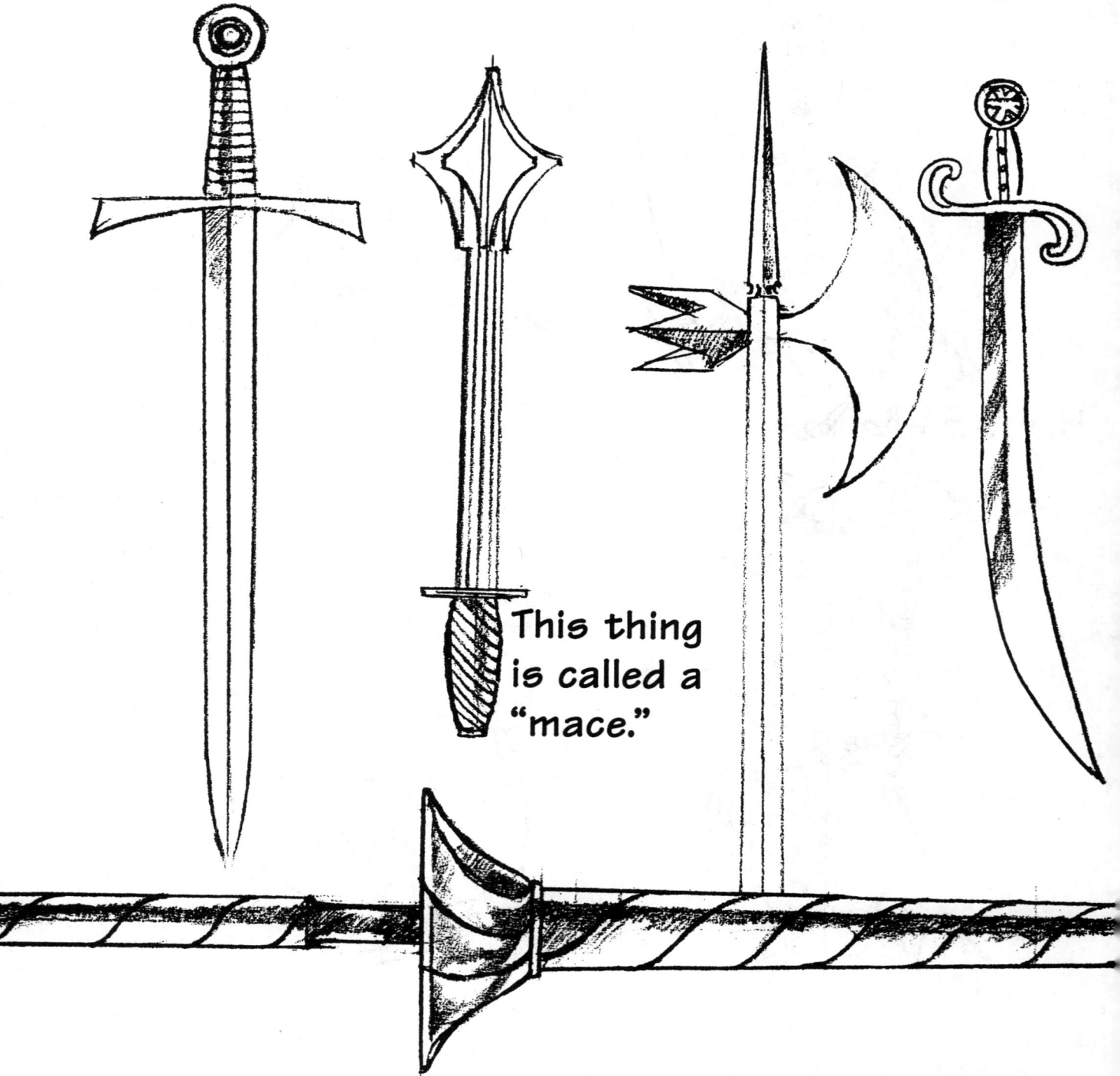

This thing
is called a
"mace."

It was common for knights to challenge one another to
a "joust." They would ride on horses towards one another carrying one of these—a jousting "lance." The object

of the woods carrying one of these! Here are a few ideas for swords.

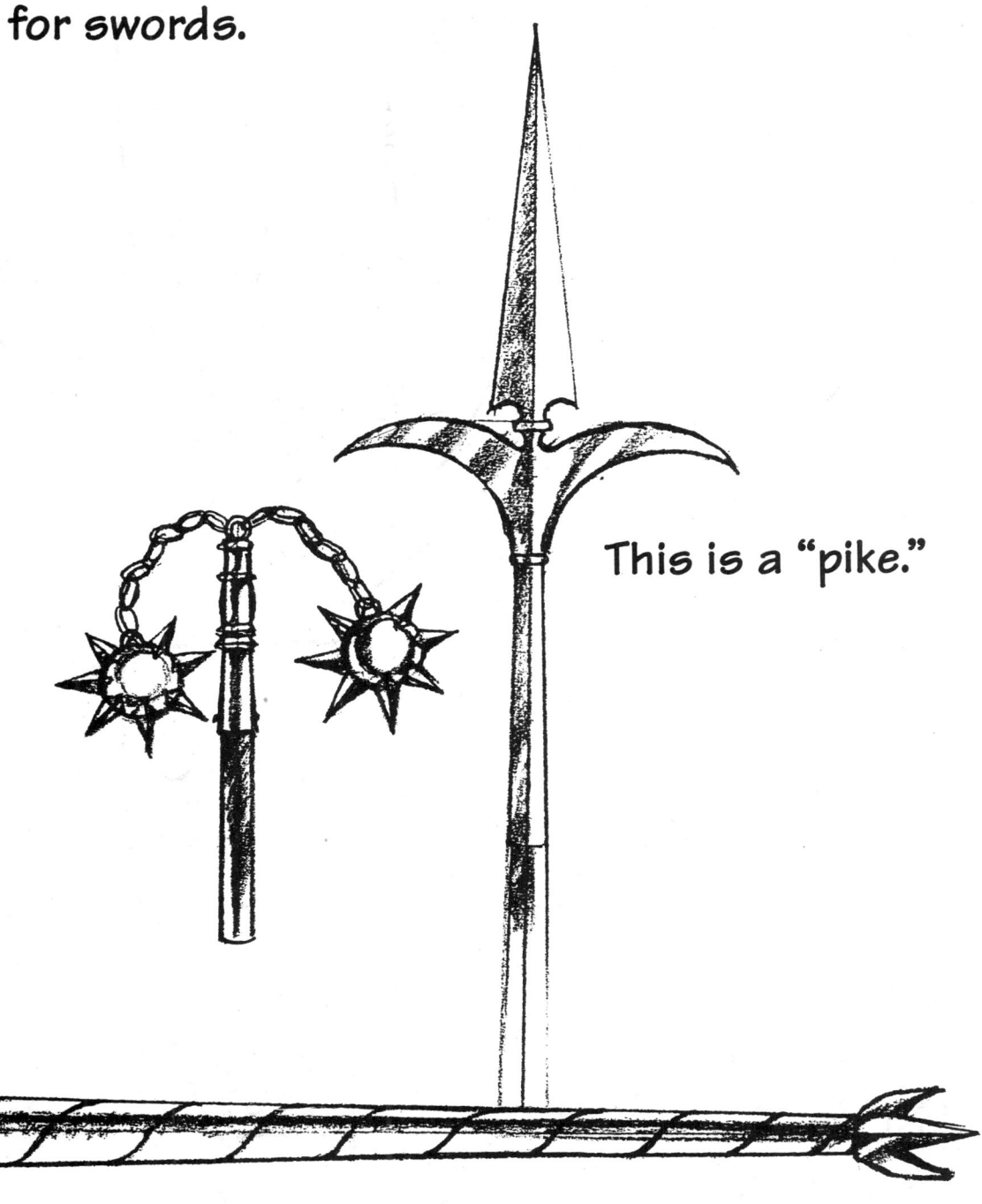

This is a "pike."

was to use the lance to knock the other knight off his horse. Ouch!

Dazzle the dragon with one of these shields. Each of these shields has a "crest" or "coat of arms."

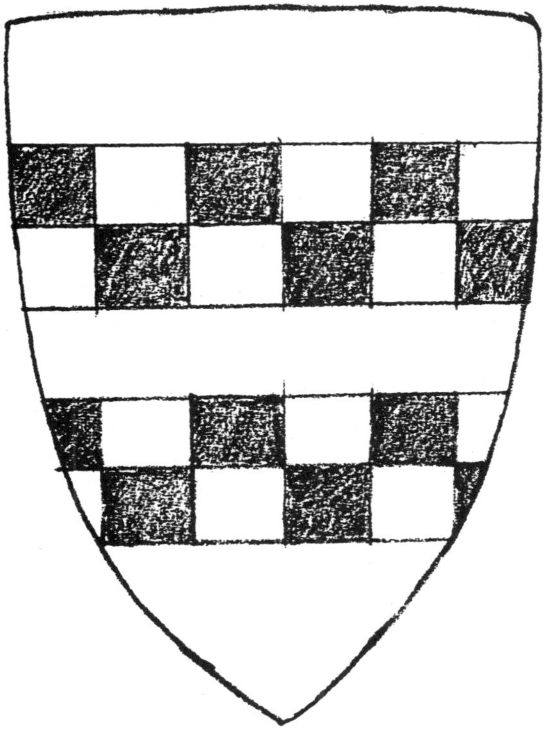

What would your special crest be?

You have a suit of armor, a sword, and a shield. All set to go battle that dragon?

Oops. Only one problem: a dragon is much faster than you—especially in all that armor. And there were no cars, bicycles, or buses back in the Middle Ages, either.

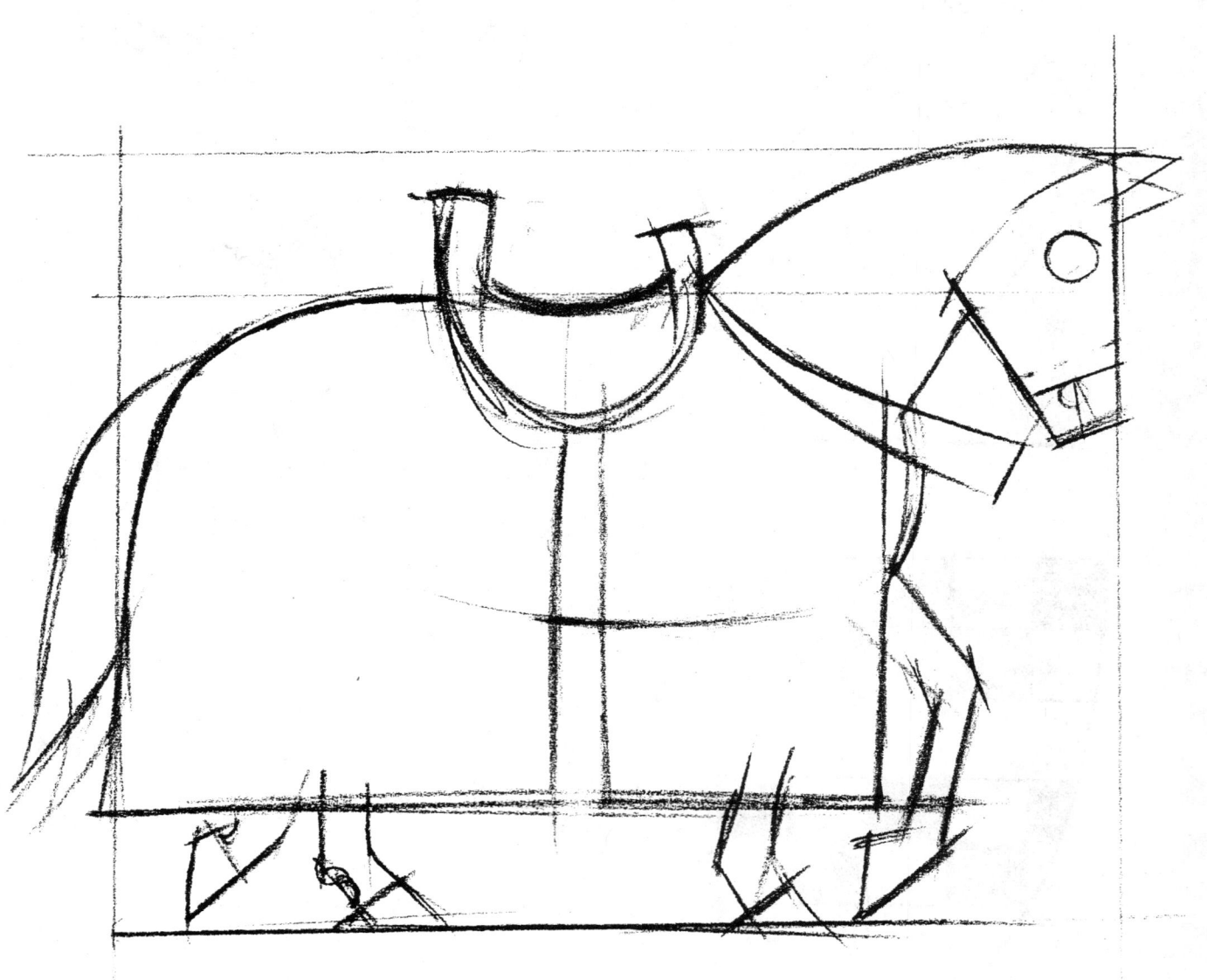

Step 1

Draw the box and guide lines. Then sketch in the main lines of a horse. Notice the high back on the saddle. That was to keep a knight from falling off his horse!

CLOPITY CLOMP, CLOPITY CLOMP. Now you can go catch that dragon!

Step 2

Decorate the horse's cloth with your crest or coat of arms.

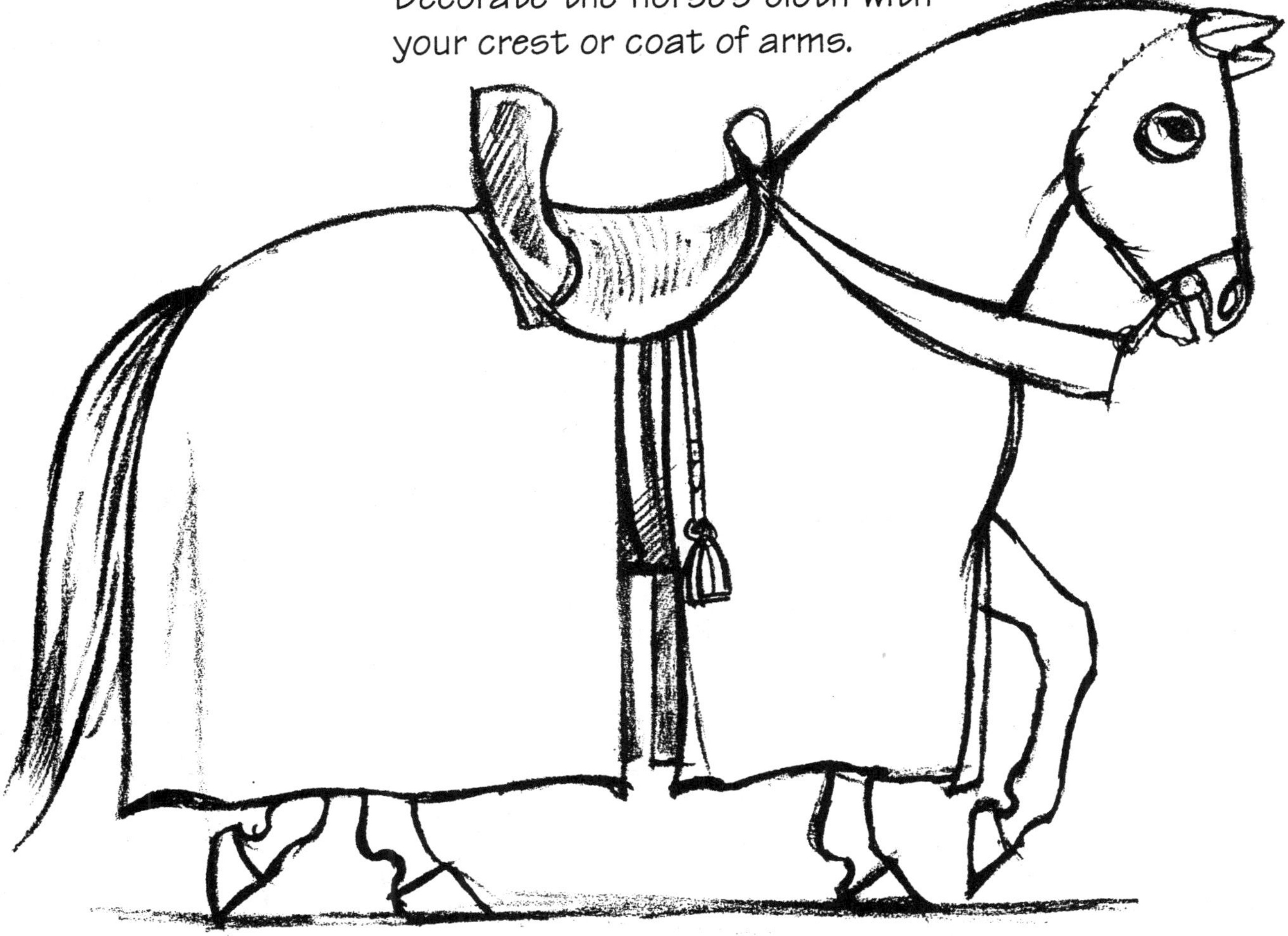

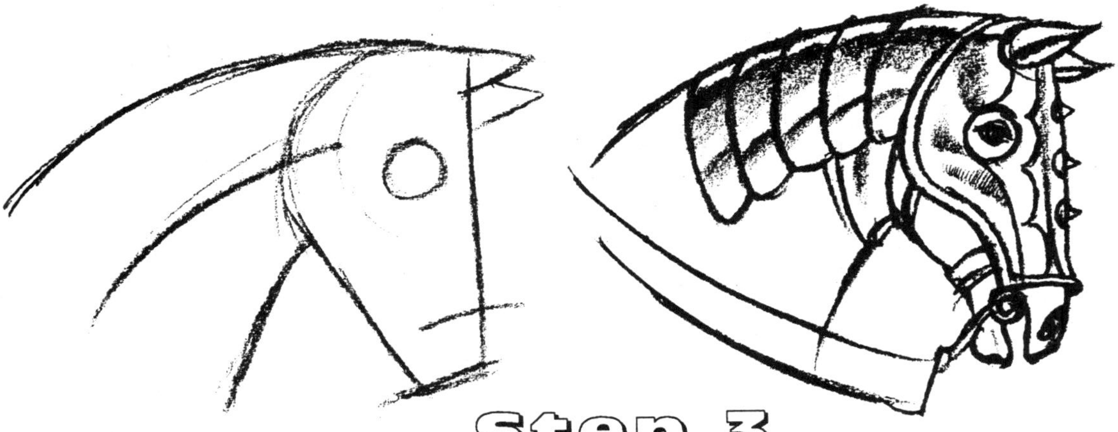

Step 3

Your horse could use some protection, too. Try adding some armor—especially around the head and neck.

All set! Now where did that dragon go? He's too big to hide. There he is!

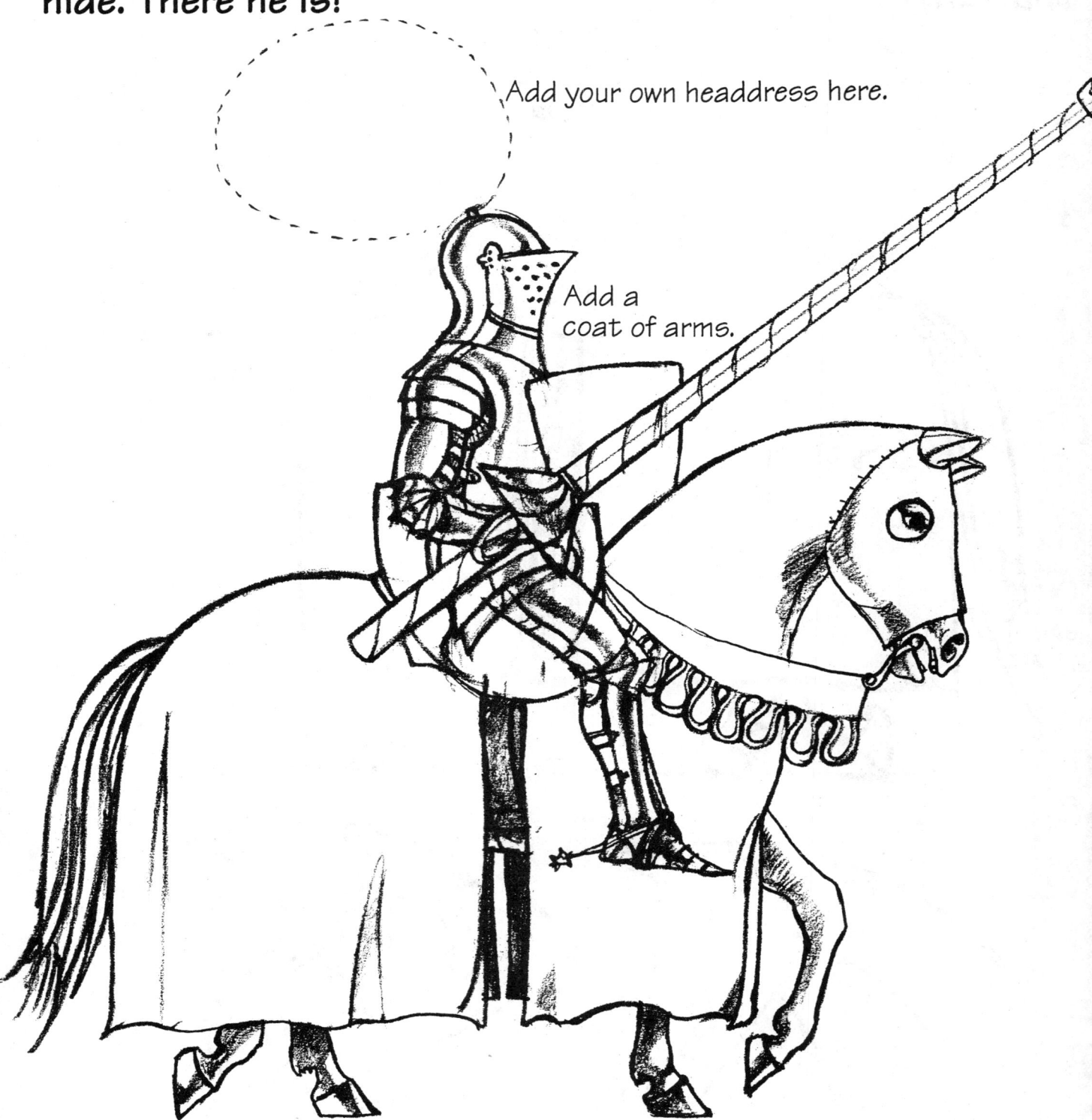

Add your own headdress here.

Add a coat of arms.

Decorate the horse with coat of arms.

Hey...who's that peeking around the door? It's the Princess of the castle!

Another thing that wasn't invented in the Middle Ages was comfortable clothes, like jeans and T-shirts. The

Step 1

Correct proportions are the most important part of figure drawing. So don't go on to Step 2 until the proportions are right.

Step 2

Try drawing this headdress—or choose another from the next page. The necklace is gold. Use a deep color for the dress—rich colors were a sign of royalty.

dresses worn by princesses were bulky and very heavy—and very very elaborate! Especially the hats...

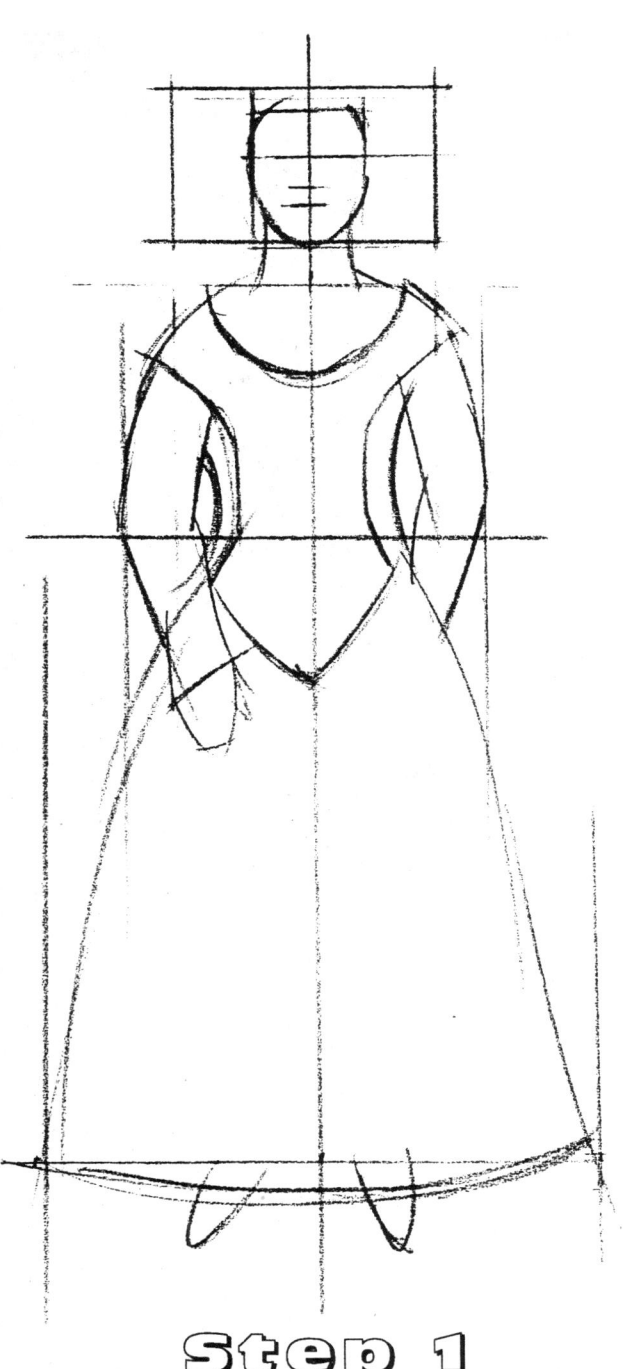

Step 1

Same as before. But this time try something a little different.

Step 2

The headress, the shoes, and the buttons on the dress were made from real gold! (You don't find outfits like that at the local mall!)

Wearing fancy headdresses was a way for a princess to show off. (Ever wonder why castles always have such high ceilings? Maybe some of these headdresses were just too TALL!)

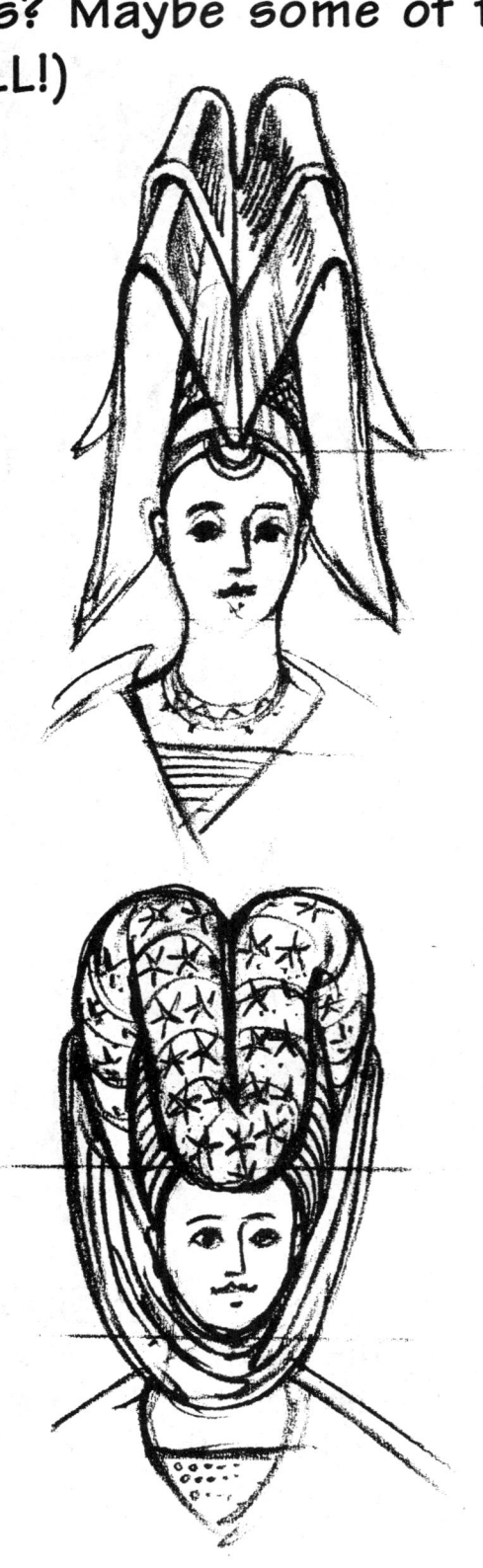

It was fashionable to have veils trailing from a headress like a tail. Color them transparent or solid.

This princess looks like the original Conehead!

Or sometimes two tails!

CHARRRRGE!!!!

Step 1

As before, first sketch the guidelines and make sure proportions are correct.
NOTE: By bending the horse's legs it looks like it's running. (The more bend in the legs, the faster it's running!)

Step 2

Add details to finish your drawing.

NOTE: See how the horse's tail is drawn more sideways than up-and-down? That makes it look like the horse is running. Same thing with the Princess's veil: drawing a curved line makes it appear that her veil is caught in the wind.

WHOA! This fire-breathing dragon is even bigger and meaner than you expected. But NO PROBLEM!

Step 1

That's right: sketch rough guidelines first, and make sure proportions are correct. See how both figures are drawn at an angle? That makes them appear as if they are leaning backwards.

Step 2

Add details to your Knight and Princess.

But the dragon doesn't look so mean anymore, does he?

Finish drawing the face, dress, and flag.

Add details to the dragon.

Add a
coat of arms.

Decorate
the banner.

Add details to the dragon.

Time to go back? NO WAY! Your adventures have just begun!